ROCKY MOUNTAIN SAFARI

A WILDLIFE DISCOVERY GUIDE

by Cathy and Gordon Illg
photographs by Wendy Shattil and Bob Rozinski

ROBERTS RINEHART PUBLISHERS

Text copyright © 1994 by Cathy and Gordon Illg
Photographs copyright © 1994 by Wendy Shattil and Bob Rozinski

Published in the United States of America
by Roberts Rinehart Publishers
Post Office Box 666, Niwot, Colorado 80544

International Standard Book Number 1-879373-79-3
Library of Congress Catalog Card Number 94-65086

Printed in Hong Kong by Colorcorp/Sing Cheong

Distributed in the United States and Canada
by Publishers Group West

Contents

Introduction   1

Elk   5
Mule Deer and White-tailed Deer   9
Moose   14
Pronghorn Antelope   18
Bighorn Sheep   21
Mountain Goat   25
Bison   28
Black Bear, Grizzly Bear   31
Gray Wolf   35
Coyote   39
Red Fox   41
Mountain Lion   44
Bobcat, Lynx   46
Weasel   48
River Otter   50
Striped Skunk   53
Marten, Fisher   55
Badger   58
Wolverine   60
Raccoon   63
Beaver   65
Porcupine   68
Muskrat   70
Yellow-bellied Marmot   72
Abert's Squirrel, Red Squirrel   74
Golden-Mantled Ground Squirrel, Chipmunk   76

Wyoming Ground Squirrel   78
Prairie Dog   80
Snowshoe Hare   82
Cottontail   84
Pika   85

Bibliography   87
About the Authors   88

INTRODUCTION

"What is man without the beasts? If all the beasts were gone, men would die from a great loneliness of spirit." Chief Seattle said that more than 150 years ago. It's a quote that gets a lot of use, and contains much truth. At least the numbers of people flocking to our national parks and wildlife refuges for a glimpse of these beasts seem to substantiate this philosophy. Judging by the traffic jams that a wildlife sighting can cause, many of us are already suffering from a loneliness of the spirit created by living apart from wildlife.

Cathy and I have always been fascinated by the natural world, and not long after moving to Colorado twelve years ago, we took up nature and wildlife photography. It's apparently a hazard related to living near the Rockies, for many newcomers we know have also fallen victim to this psychosis. As tenderfeet in the world of wildlife photography, our most time-consuming problem was simply finding suitable subjects. And other wildlife photographers were seldom willing to talk about their favorite locations. We heard things like, "Rocky Mountain National Park is good for bighorns." Sure it is, but *where* in Rocky Mountain National Park, and just as important, *when*?

After five or six years of searching the Rockies for cooperative wildlife we felt we were getting some pretty darn good images. That is until we tried to make some money at it. In 1988 though, we got one of our biggest breaks when we took a photography class from Wendy Shattil and Robert Rozinski. After seeing some of their photos it was easy to understand why ours weren't selling particularly well.

Before seeing Wendy and Bob's work we would have said that our photos could adequately illustrate this book. And they could; and they would be just that—adequate. Wendy and Bob's photos however, portray the animals in situations few people get to see, or in light that is nothing short of magical.

Looking back on our rocky start in the wildlife photo-journalism business, we agree that the most frustrating thing was simply finding the animals. For visitors with a limited amount of time the task must appear even more formidable. I remember photographing a herd of remarkably tolerant mule deer after several very unproductive weekends in other locations, and Cathy commented, "If only there was a guidebook describing places like this." That was the birth of the idea for this book. We can't count the number of times we wished for such a resource.

The purpose of this book is to provide information on mammals of the Rocky Mountains, and guide the reader to the best places to view them, especially within Rocky Mountain National Park. It also covers productive wildlife-viewing locations within the Rocky Mountain states of Colorado, Wyoming, Montana, and Idaho.

Many visitors drive through the national parks, see few animals, and leave thinking the place was overrated. For viewing many species, being there at the right time is as important as being in the right location. Most big game species are much more active in the early morning and late afternoon than they are during the middle of the day, and wildlife-watching excursions should be planned accordingly.

Once the animals are found, treat them with respect. No photo, even for a professional photographer, is worth interrupting or interfering in the animal's life. Don't feed the animals. Even if what you're feeding them is nutritional, it may concentrate unnatural numbers of a species in a certain area, and the animals will come to depend upon handouts for survival. Baby animals should be left alone. Even when they appear to be abandoned, their mother is usually nearby keeping an eye on them. Don't try to sneak up on wild animals. Their senses are so keen that the idea is ludicrous.

When approaching an animal, you do, however, have to pay attention, and approach only when your subject will tolerate it. Move slowly, and in a zig-zag pattern toward your subject. Give the animal plenty of space. If it stops what it's doing to watch you, you're probably too close. Wait a bit to see if it resumes its activity before approaching closer.

Understand that most published photos were taken using a blind to bring the animals in close, or were taken with a lens resembling a bazooka. To duplicate those photos, you will need similar equipment. Trying to make up for professional technique and equipment by approaching the animals closely puts you in danger, and/or frightens the animal away.

Another professional photographic trick is the use of tame or captive animals to obtain intimate behavior shots and close-ups. Almost every cat photo published, including the ones in this guide, involves an animal in such a controlled situation. Professional wildlife photographer Leonard Lee Rue III once said, "Show me a picture of a mountain lion, and I'll tell you its name."

The mammals included in this guide are by no means the only mammals that exist in this part of the Rocky Mountains. In fact, two entire orders (bats and insectivores) have been omitted. The species represented in this guide are a combination of the mammals a visitor is most likely to see, and the ones most visitors want to see.

May this guide help ease your loneliness of spirit as doing the research for it has helped ease ours.

ELK
(Cervus elaphus)

Elk bugling is a unique phenomena in North America. No other mammal on the continent uses this kind of vocalization to attract a mate or intimidate a foe.
—Alan Christensen, wildlife biologist, United States Forest Service, Montana

Early one January morning Cathy and I were observing a good-size herd of bull elk on the outskirts of Estes Park, Colorado, and were surprised to hear antlers clashing. We'd always heard that once the rut ended in late fall the bulls quit this kind of nonsense. Forty feet away from us, though, several groups were wrestling with locked antlers, including a threesome that made an impressive but dangerous-looking triangle. For the most part they were young bulls, but there were two large ones that went through the group, methodically and quickly thrashing each of the youngsters.

We relearned a lesson that morning. You can seldom predict what animals will do at any given time, and even the "experts" can't explain some of their behavior. Just be thankful for the opportunity to experience it.

ELK FACTS

- Elk belong to the deer family (Cervidae).

- Males can weigh up to 1,000 pounds, and have large branching antlers. Females weigh about half as much and have no antlers.
- Like all deer, elk shed their antlers during the winter, and grow new ones during the summer. Antlers differ from horns in that antlers are made of bone, and are shed each year. Horns are made from modified hair and are never shed.
- Males are called bulls, females are cows, and young are calves.
- Breeding season (called the rut or rutting season) lasts from early September to early November. Elk are considered the most polygamous deer in the world, and the males breed with as many females as possible. Mature bulls bugle throughout the rut.
- Calves, usually one but sometimes twins, are born in the first weeks of June.
- Elk are also called Wapiti, a Shawnee word meaning "white rump" or "white deer." In Europe, elk (*elch* in German) refers to the animal we call moose.
- Elk were the most numerous deer on the continent before the white man's arrival, and they ranged from ocean to ocean. Except for a few reserves, elk are now restricted to mountainous regions from the Rockies west to the Pacific.
- Aspen bark is a favored food in winter when other food sources are buried under snow, and elk-scarred aspen are a common sight where elk range. It is also thought that aspen bark contains a mild anesthetic that may aid the females during calving.

THE RUT

The spectacle put on by elk during the rut is one of the most impressive in the animal world. Between establishing dominance, chasing off rivals and gathering, guarding, and servicing a harem of up to 60 cows, an observer is guaranteed lots of action. During the rut, a dominant bull may not sleep or eat for days at a time.

At this time of year bull elk have trouble distinguishing between real rivals and innocent bystanders. In a national wildlife refuge in Nebraska where remnant herds of elk and longhorn cattle were kept together, we watched a large bull elk chase a longhorn bull away from the elk's harem. The longhorn bull outweighed the elk by about 1,000 pounds. I never realized those longhorns could move so quickly, but then a 30-pound aggregation of daggers attached to an angry bull elk can be a tremendous incentive to look for greener pastures. On a ranch in northern Oregon, a bull elk scared away a Hereford bull, and stood guard over the rancher's domestic cows.

Elk, especially the bulls, are potentially dangerous. If they'll drive off animals as large as domestic bulls, they may not hesitate to skewer a wildlife-watcher who approaches too closely. A photographer's tripod can resemble an impressive set of antlers, and provoke an attack. Few people have actually been injured by elk, and if an elk does charge, it is usually content to just chase the intruder away. The elk have more important things to do. Because of their near-constant activity during rutting season they spend little time eating, and the dominant bulls will lose about 100 pounds in a few short weeks. If they can't replace that weight before the onset of winter, they probably won't see another spring.

WHERE TO FIND ELK

ROCKY MOUNTAIN NATIONAL PARK, CO—Although there are many places in Colorado where elk can be seen, Rocky Mountain National Park offers some of the best opportunities for photography. The park is home to about 3,000 elk during summer and about 1,200 during winter.

Summer: Although we've seen bulls in the meadow near the Aspenglen Campground during the summer, most of the bulls are at higher altitudes at this time of year. Good places to see them are near Poudre Lake, Medicine Bow Curve, and below the Fall River Pass Visitor Center.

Fall, Winter & Spring: When the rut is at its height (mid-September to mid-October) the best places to see elk are Horseshoe Park, Moraine Park, Beaver Meadows, and meadows like Harbison along the Colorado River on the west side of the park. The best times to see them are early morning and late afternoon. The east side of Rocky Mountain National Park is crowded at this time of year, especially in the evening as visitors gather to watch and listen to the elk. If you don't mind a short walk, the trail from Hollowell Park is also good for elk this time of year, and can help you escape the worst of the crowd. The elk will remain close to these valleys until the snows release the high country in early summer. During the late fall and winter another good viewing location is the golf course in the nearby town of Estes Park. The golf course is on the east side of town and on the north side of Lake Estes.

ELK MEADOW, EVERGREEN, CO—This can also be a good place, because as part of the Jefferson County Open Space system the animals here are also protected. This 1,140-acre parcel of wildlife habitat is just north of Evergreen off Highway 74.

COLORADO STATEWIDE. Good wintering areas include Axial Basin on Road 17 west of Craig and south of Lay in northwest Colorado; the viewing area at the Holy Cross Ranger District office just south of the junction of I-70 and Highway 24 west of Vail; west of Trinidad in southeast Colorado on County Road 13 from Stonewall south to the New Mexico state line; Gunnison State Wildlife Area west of Gunnison and north of Highway 50 on Road 726.

MUSSELSHELL MEADOWS, ID—The meadows are a marshy habitat surrounded by dense coniferous forest, and during the spring and summer elk are common here. From the town of Weippe in north-central Idaho drive east 8 miles to Peterson Corners. Turn right on Road 100. After 4 miles turn left on Road 540 and continue for .5 miles to a parking lot. The meadow is encircled by roads, so wildlife viewing may be conducted from a vehicle.

SAND CREEK WILDLIFE MANAGEMENT AREA, ID—Sand Creek is winter range for 2,500 elk. From St. Anthony, southeast of Yellowstone National Park, take Middle Street north through town. At the U.S. Forest Service office turn east. After 1.5 miles turn left onto Sand Creek Road, and continue 16.5 miles to Sand Creek Ponds. Vehicle access is restricted in some of this area to protect the animals. Check with the Idaho Department of Fish and Game (208-624-7065).

NATIONAL BISON RANGE, MT—This refuge northeast of Missoula can provide opportunities for elk viewing at any time of year.

NORTHERN YELLOWSTONE WINTER RANGE, MT—This area just north of Yellowstone National Park, along Highway 89 between Gardiner and Corwin Springs, and the gravel road between Gardiner and Jardine, is winter habitat for 20,000 elk, the largest herd in the country.

NATIONAL ELK REFUGE, WY—For sheer numbers of elk (up to 10,000 in mid-winter) take a winter sleigh ride through this refuge between Grand Teton National Park and Jackson, Wyoming. Depending on when the snows come, the elk are usually here in large numbers from Thanksgiving through Easter. Call (307) 733-9212.

YELLOWSTONE NATIONAL PARK, WY—There is no better place than Yellowstone for photographing the elk rut, and the army of photographers present in the fall is testimony to that fact. The Mammoth area, the meadows just west of Madison Junction, and the meadows around Norris Campground offer some of the most accessible elk herds in the park.

Mule Deer

MULE DEER
(Odocoileus hemionus)
WHITE-TAILED DEER
(Odocoileus virginianus)

When do the deer turn into elk?
—Tourist overheard at Rocky Mountain National Park

We had moved slowly, looking around at the horizon, pretending not to be interested in the mule deer we were approaching. Some of the deer got up from where they had been resting, but to our surprise they moved toward us. Almost immediately we were in the middle of the herd. Two small bucks—a couple of fork-horns—started antler wrestling within 30 feet of us.

Soon the herd had moved on and we were outsiders again. We felt strangely elated as we walked back to the car. For a few minutes we had been part of the wild herd, and it was almost hard to return to the civilized world.

DEER FACTS
- Both mule deer and white-tailed deer belong to the deer family (Cervidae).

- Although they appear similar, deer do not turn into elk. They are separate species.
- Males are called bucks, females are does, and young are fawns.
- In both species the males have branching antlers that are shed each winter and regrown each summer. The females do not have antlers.
- White-tails are generally slimmer, have longer necks and shorter ears than mule deer. The tail of a white-tail is dark above and white beneath. The white seldom shows until the animal runs. As it flees it lifts its tail, making it look like a waving, white flag. This is where the expression "high-tailing it" comes from. The antlers of a white-tail buck consist of a main beam that curls forward and secondary tines, or points, that sprout up from the main beam.
- Mule deer are stockier and have much longer ears than white-tails. A mule deer's tail is white with a dark tip, and the tail is not particularly evident when the animal flees. The antlers of a mule deer buck split into forks, and tend to grow up and out rather than forward.
- The breeding season for both species can last from late October to mid-December. Bucks may have single does, or harems with usually fewer than 10 does.
- Fawns are usually born in June, and if it is the doe's first offspring, she will have a single fawn. Thereafter, she will always have twins, or occasionally triplets.
- According to many authorities, fawns have little scent, making it hard for predators to find them. There appears to be no scientific evidence to support this belief, however. The fawns are well camouflaged, and their spots allow them to blend into the sun-dappled forest floor, but a 1977 study for the Colorado Division of Wildlife still found a 67% fawn mortality rate.
- A fawn spends most of its first three days alone, lying motionless under cover, waiting for its mother to return. Its mother only returns to nurse it several times a day to lessen the chance of a predator following her back to the fawn. If you find a fawn, leave it alone and don't touch it. There is little likelihood that it is an orphan, and if you do touch it, predators can find it by your scent.
- Although they are the most common big game animal in North America, in the Rockies, white-tail deer are not nearly as common as mule deer.
- In 1948, the white-tail deer was declared extirpated (locally extinct as opposed to worldwide) in Colorado. In the years after World War II,

white-tails have colonized all of the major river bottoms in the eastern part of the state. Mule deer were common in many of these areas, and white-tails have now forced them out.

• White-tails prefer the denser vegetation of river corridors at the mountain's base. Mule deer can be found from alpine tundra to the plains.

WHERE TO FIND MULE DEER
ROCKY MOUNTAIN NATIONAL PARK, CO

Summer: The deer are spread out this time of year and can be anywhere from Estes Park or Grand Lake to the top of Trail Ridge. The biggest bucks tend to stay close to timberline during the summer. Medicine Bow Curve can be a good place to find them.

Fall and Winter: When the weather turns cold the east side of the park is most productive, for it's lower and gets less snow. This makes it easier for the deer to find food. The stretch of road that goes from the Beaver Meadows Visitor Center past Beaver Meadows and over the shoulder of Deer Ridge is one of the best drives in the park for sighting mule deer. Don't overlook other areas though, for the entire foothills section of the park has lots of deer this time of year.

BILLY CREEK STATE WILDLIFE AREA/RIDGEWAY STATE PARK, CO—This area between Ridgeway and Montrose is good for viewing deer all year, but winter concentrates even more of the animals in the area.

BOULDER MOUNTAIN PARKS, BOULDER, CO—The parks are a series of open-space areas along the foothills west of Boulder, Colorado, and are maintained by Boulder County. In some places the deer have become used to people. The grounds of the National Center for Atmospheric Research is one good place to see them, but there is no parking allowed along the road. You have to wait for the deer to come to the parking lot, which happens frequently, or be willing to hike.

GREAT SAND DUNES NATIONAL MONUMENT, CO—Mule deer have become so numerous here that some have become a nuisance. Sadly, the surest way to attract these picnic-ground deer is to rattle a potato chip bag. Please, don't feed the wildlife. While the does and young can be seen any time of year along the main road, the big bucks are rarely seen this low until fall or winter.

LORY STATE PARK, CO—This park, a few miles northwest of Ft. Collins, is also in foothills habitat and has numerous deer, especially from fall to spring.

ROCKY MOUNTAIN ARSENAL, DENVER, CO—The arsenal has become part of the national wildlife refuge system. When its cleanup is completed, it may be the best place to see large mule deer bucks in the country. Unfortunately, it is not yet open to the public on a regular basis. Free double-decker bus tours are given every weekend, and you are almost guaranteed to see lots of deer. Call (303) 289-0132 for information on tours.

BEAR LAKE NATIONAL WILDLIFE REFUGE, ID—Hundreds of mule deer winter on the slopes of Merkley Mountain. From Montpelier in extreme southeast Idaho go 3 miles west on Highway 89, and turn left onto Bear Lake County Airport Road. Continue 5 miles to the refuge entrance road.

BOISE RIVER WILDLIFE MANAGEMENT AREA, ID—Over 6,000 mule deer winter on these sagebrush-covered foothills. Four miles east of Boise take Idaho 21. Viewing begins here and continues along Idaho 21 for the next 16 miles.

White-tailed Deer

CRATERS OF THE MOON NATIONAL MONUMENT, ID—Located in south-central Idaho, the lava formations provide a unique setting for wildlife viewing.

EDNESS KIMBALL WILKINS STATE PARK, WY—Mule deer can often be found in drainage bottoms or along the riparian edges of this state park, which is about 10 miles east of Casper on U.S. 20/26.

WHERE TO FIND WHITE-TAILS

COLORADO ROCKIES—The best places to find white-tails are near protected riparian areas in the eastern foothills. In the Denver area, Cherry Creek State Recreation Area, Chatfield State Park, east of Boulder along Boulder Creek, and Rocky Mountain Arsenal (see notation under mule deer) have good populations of white-tails.

CHAIN OF LAKES, ID—White-tails are common along this 13-mile stretch of the Coeur d'Alene River, which is bordered by shallow lakes and wetlands. From Coeur d'Alene in northern Idaho take I-90 east for 18 miles and turn south on Idaho 3. The Chain of Lakes area begins in 3 miles.

CLARK FORK RIVER DELTA AT LAKE PEND OREILLE, ID—See section under Moose for directions.

GLACIER NATIONAL PARK, MT—The lower elevations of the park have strong populations of white-tails, but the vegetation is dense, and seeing the deer may be difficult. Often, the best places to find them are around campgrounds and lodges.

KELLY ISLAND, MT—Kelly Island is a semi-wild park on the west edge of Missoula in northwest Montana. Access to the island itself is by boat, but white-tails are often seen between the parking lot and the shore, and even in the surrounding neighborhood.

NATIONAL BISON RANGE, MT—White-tails are often seen along the riparian area on the north side of this refuge in northwest Montana.

EDNESS KIMBALL WILKINS STATE PARK, WY—Look for white-tails feeding along the Platte River. For directions, see notation under mule deer.

MOOSE
(Alces alces)

Anyone who is mistaken for a moose and shot, is better off dead anyway.
—A wildlife researcher commenting on how attractive moose are

Cathy and I were up early to watch the sunrise wash over the peaks of the Grand Tetons, but a drama of another kind soon had us captivated. A large bull moose and a much smaller bull were interested in a cow moose that had a large calf with her. The cow was not ready to mate, and she was trying to get the message across to the large bull.

After some minutes of attempting to mount her, the big bull gave up and lay down in the shade. The smaller bull then tried sneaking around the willows to come at the cow from the other side. This didn't fool the large bull, and he was standing near the cow, thrashing his antlers against the willows, when the smaller bull finished its sneaky approach. Undaunted, the smaller bull immediately chased the calf out of a choice stand of willows. It's always nice to have someone smaller to pick on.

MOOSE FACTS
- Moose are the largest animal in the deer family (Cervidae).
- There are four different subspecies in North America, and all of them are big. The shoulders of the largest subspecies, the Alaskan, will be taller than a full-size van. A large male can weigh 1,800 pounds, and females can weigh up to 800 pounds. In the Rockies, a bull can weigh up to 1,300 pounds.
- The males have huge palmate antlers (shaped like a hand with fingers spread) that can spread more than six feet across. These antlers are shed in the winter, and are regrown the following summer. The females do not have antlers.
- Males are called bulls, females are cows, and young are calves.
- The breeding season lasts from mid-September to mid-October.
- Large bulls will fight other bulls for breeding rights. The bulls do not keep harems but, after mating with one female, will look for others.
- Moose are excellent swimmers.
- Willow leaves and twigs form a large part of a moose's diet, as do many aquatic plants. Moose will actually dive underwater for them. Many aquatic plants concentrate minerals in their tissues, and moose need these minerals for antler growth and for healthy muscle and nerve operation.
- A moose's joints are specially articulated as an adaptation to its habitat. Because of this adaptation, a moose's rear legs pull straight up rather than swinging forward. This allows the moose to move through deep water and mud, or deep snow, very rapidly.
- Moose are probably the second most dangerous animal in the Rockies. Like bison (the most dangerous animal in the Rockies), they are large enough to go where they want to, even if a tourist is standing in the way. Rutting bulls and cows with calves should be given plenty of room.

WHERE TO FIND MOOSE
COLORADO—Historically, moose occasionally wandered into Colorado, but they did not remain in any great numbers. With some help from the Division of Wildlife, moose are now residents and are doing quite well. North Park near Walden (north-central Colorado) received the first

transplanted moose—a dozen from Utah in 1978, and a dozen more the following January from Wyoming.

Moose are great wanderers, and from North Park they've colonized much of the north-central part of the state, including Rocky Mountain National Park. Look for them in the Kawuneeche Valley where the Colorado River flows through the west side of Rocky Mountain National Park.

Probably the best place in Colorado to find moose is near where they were originally released. There are now more than 600 moose roaming North Park, and from June through the end of October a good place to look for them is along the Illinois River southeast of Rand.

The Laramie River Road from Glendevy south to Highway 14 can also be good for moose-watching. In the years to come the area around Creede in southwest Colorado may become a moose hotspot, for they have recently been introduced there.

LAKE PEND OREILLE, ID—Moose are common in both the Pack River and the Clark Fork River delta areas. Access to these areas is off Idaho 200 east of Sandpoint in northern Idaho.

LOCHSA RIVER CANYON, ID—During summer and fall the salt licks at Elk Summit Cabin can be an excellent place to view moose. Take U.S. Highway 12 to the Powell Ranger Station 65 miles east of Lowell in north-central Idaho. From the ranger station (near mile post 162) go south for 2 miles and turn west on Road 111 and in 3 miles take the right fork (Road 360) and continue 12 miles to Elk Summit.

SAND CREEK WILDLIFE MANAGEMENT AREA, ID—This area is winter range for some 200 moose. See Elk section for directions.

GLACIER NATIONAL PARK, MT—The "Moose Country" pullout on Going-to-the-Sun Road between Lake McDonald and Logan Pass is one of the few easily accessible places where moose can be seen.

RED ROCKS NATIONAL WILDLIFE REFUGE, MT—This refuge west of Yellowstone National Park on the Montana-Idaho border is a good place to find moose. In fact, we were awakened one night in September by one swinging its antlers against a tree outside our tent at 4:00 a.m. The best areas are in the willows near Upper Lake Campground and along the south shore of Upper Lake. Before visiting this refuge in the fall though, check when hunting season is.

GRAND TETON NATIONAL PARK, WY—Willow Flats on the east side of Jackson Lake; along the Buffalo River near Moran Junction; and Blacktail Ponds Overlook.

YELLOWSTONE NATIONAL PARK, WY—Indian Creek Campground especially in the spring; meadows south of Canyon Junction; Hayden Valley; Willow Park; and just inside the northeast entrance to the park. We've also seen them in timber just south of Dunraven Pass in late summer.

PRONGHORN ANTELOPE
(Antilocapra americana)

If pronghorn ran marathons they would complete the 26 mile course in 40 minutes.
—Rachel Nowak, "The Pronghorn's Prowess," *Discover* 12/92

It was a sunless morning, and the invigorating scent of damp earth permeated the air. Low clouds amplified the constant rumble of hooves pounding across the grassland. It was mid-September at the National Bison Range in northwest Montana, and the pronghorn bucks had one thing in mind—mating.

The dominant buck in the herd we were observing was doing his best to chase off half-a-dozen would-be suitors, and keep a group of does together at the same time. He would chase rivals for a half-mile or more and come trotting back a minute later, only to take off again after another rival or a doe. Any time the dominant buck's attention was elsewhere, the other bucks were checking to see if any of the does had come into estrus (were ready to mate). Once, the dominant buck stopped within 20 feet of our vehicle, blowing hard. He seemed to stop out of indecision about his next target, and not because he was winded. Within seconds he was off chasing another buck.

PRONGHORN FACTS

- Authorities are split as to whether pronghorns belong to the family Bovidae (cows, goats, sheep) or to their own family, Antilocapridae.
- Pronghorns are the only animal with a true horn whose horny sheath is shed after the breeding season, leaving only two small bony cores sticking up from its head.
- There are many animals with branching *antlers*, but the pronghorn is the only known animal with branching *horns*.
- Adult males can weigh up to 140 pounds, and females slightly less.
- Both sexes have horns, but the horns of mature males are much larger than those of the females.
- Males are called bucks, females are does, and young are fawns.
- Breeding season lasts about two weeks in mid-September. Bucks fight for dominance, and gather harems of does.
- Fawns are born in late May or early June. Twins are common, and triplets happen occasionally.
- Pronghorns flare their white rump patches when alarmed to alert other members of the herd.
- Several Ice Ages ago there were 13 species of pronghorns on this continent. Now there is only one.
- Even though famous for being the second-fastest land animal, the pronghorn's running abilities are actually second to none. A cheetah may have a slightly higher top speed (70 mph as opposed to 61 mph), but a cheetah would not stand a chance of catching a pronghorn. A cheetah can only keep its speed up for several hundred yards. A pronghorn can run at 45 mph for three or four miles, and at 35 mph for hours.
- A pronghorn's windpipe is twice the diameter of a human's. It has been reported that a pronghorn's leg bones are stronger than a cow's, though only a quarter as large.
- Pronghorns have the largest eyes of any North American ungulate (hoofed mammal) in proportion to its body size. Its vision is equivalent to a human looking through 8-power binoculars. Its eyes also protrude to the sides, giving the animal an additional advantage. Unlike most mammals, pronghorns do not have a blind spot directly behind them. The pronghorns' eyes protrude enough to allow them to see backwards and forwards, and although they actually can only see movement behind them, it's a big help in alerting them to predators.
- Pronghorns are very curious, and hunters from the Stone Age to the present have taken advantage of this to lure them within striking distance.

- Some 60 to 75 million pronghorns roamed the west when the prairie ecosystem was still intact. By 1918 only 10,000 remained. Today, about 750,000 live on the sagebrush flats and open prairies that still exist.
- Sagebrush is a staple of their diet, especially during the winter, making pronghorns members of a select group of animals that can digest sagebrush.
- The biggest threat to pronghorns today is fences. A pronghorn can leap across a 27-foot-wide pit, but a three-foot barbed-wire fence may as well be the Great Wall of China. We watched one try three times to clear a 32-inch fence. A pronghorn's legs are not adapted for jumping high, and a pronghorn will go under a fence rather than over it, if at all possible. In severe winter weather, fences can kill hundreds or even thousands of pronghorns by preventing them from reaching winter pastures.

WHERE TO FIND PRONGHORN

CRAIG, CO—The sagebrush flats north and west of Craig in northwest Colorado have numerous pronghorn.

GREAT SAND DUNES NATIONAL MONUMENT, CO—The area around the monument probably has the most human-tolerant herd of pronghorns in Colorado, but there are not many here, and they may be hard to find.

NORTH PARK, CO—In the north-central part of the state near Walden.

SAN LUIS VALLEY, CO—Especially the area around Saguache, and near or on the golf course west of Crestone in south-central Colorado.

BIRCH CREEK VALLEY, ID—Driving on Idaho 28 north of its junction with Idaho 22 in eastern Idaho often yields close views of pronghorns.

MORGAN CREEK, ID—From Challis in central Idaho drive north on U.S. 93 for 8.3 miles. Turn left on Forest Road 55, and look for pronghorns for the next 5 miles.

NATIONAL BISON RANGE, MT—The pronghorn herd here is often near the road that visitors are restricted to. For photographers the only drawback is that some of the animals have colored tags on their ears.

YELLOWSTONE NATIONAL PARK, WY—There are often very tolerant pronghorns between Gardiner and Mammoth on the north side of the park. Pronghorns are also often seen in the Lamar Valley.

BIGHORN SHEEP
(Ovis canadensis)

There are two types of bighorn sheep, the long-horned and the short-horned.
—A visitor to Rocky Mountain National Park overheard instructing her friend

Our gloved fingers were cold and aching, and clouds of condensation rose as oohs and ahs came from the crowd of roadside spectators. But discomforts were overlooked, for bighorns were beside the road just east of the Fall River entrance to Rocky Mountain National Park; their chocolate brown winter coats stood out vividly against the fresh snow as they used their hooves to uncover hidden vegetation.

CRACK! Every human head jerked up searching for the source of the sudden noise. The feeding bighorns never even lifted theirs, for it was a sound they knew well: two rams were deciding which one was dominant. The challenger would lay its head on the other's back, and with a stiff front leg, kick the challengee in the abdomen. The two rams would then separate, turn, and crash head-to-head. Sometimes they would appear to be peacefully eating, and almost simultaneously, they would wheel toward each other on their hind legs and smash their heads together again. To the delight of spectators lining the road a hundred feet below, the rams had a devil of a time deciding who was boss, and the sound of their battle echoed through the valley for more than an hour.

BIGHORN FACTS

- Bighorn sheep are in the same family as cows, sheep and goats (Bovidae).
- Males can weigh up to 275 pounds, and females up to 150 pounds.
- Males are called rams, females are ewes, and young are lambs.
- Bighorns have true horns that are never shed, similar to bison and mountain goats.
- Bighorns are not divided into long-horned and short-horned species. Both sexes have horns. The horns of the females are slender, short, and only slightly curved. The males' horns can be massive, and may curve around in a complete 360-degree arc. Males with such large horns often have broken tips, and it has been speculated that they break the tips off on purpose so the horns don't interfere with their peripheral vision.
- Breeding season is mid-November to mid-December. The rams do not form harems, but chase after individual ewes as they come into estrus (are ready to mate). Winning a head-butting duel is not a deciding factor in which rams get to mate.
- Lambs, usually one but occasionally twins, are born at the end of May or the beginning of June.
- Bighorns have a double cranium with an inch of spongy material between to cushion the shock of butting heads.
- Bighorns depend on their keen eyesight to warn them of predators, and if their habitat is full of dense brush it can hurt the sheep in two ways: it makes it easier for mountain lions to prey upon them; and the continuous stress of not being able to see well often leads to disease in the sheep. Division of Wildlife personnel in Colorado have been fighting this effect by manually removing the brush and with controlled burns. Both Waterton and Poudre Canyons in Colorado have been treated in this way.
- During the winter, bighorns prefer south-facing slopes, because the snow melts more quickly.
- Bighorns have favorite places where they literally eat the dirt. They do this for the minerals. In the winter they will often lick the roads for the salt used in snow removal.

WHERE TO FIND BIGHORNS
ROCKY MOUNTAIN NATIONAL PARK, CO

Fall and Winter: Highway 34 just east of the Fall River Entrance to Rocky Mountain National Park remains one of the best places to see bighorns. You will be fined if caught climbing the hill to get closer to the sheep, but the sheep often come right down to the road.

Spring and Summer: Sheep Lakes in Horseshoe Park are often visited by the sheep because of the mineral-rich soil there. The crater is the most reliable place to find the sheep during mid-summer. Here the ewes and lambs spend the warm summer days among the meadows and rocky cliffs. The crater is usually closed to the public until July to give the sheep privacy during lambing. The trail to the crater begins across the highway from Poudre Lake and takes the visitor above 11,000 feet. It is only about 1 1/2 miles long, but it is steep.

BIG BEND CAMPGROUND, CO—Bighorns are often seen on the rocky slopes on the north side of Highway 14 in the Poudre River Canyon west of Ft. Collins.

GEORGETOWN, CO—The Colorado Division of Wildlife has constructed an observation tower with coin-operated scopes on the shore of Georgetown Lake. A large herd of bighorn can often be seen during the fall, winter, and spring on the steep slopes north of I-70.

WATERTON CANYON, CO—Access to this canyon is off of Highway 121 south of Highway C-470 on the southwest edge of the Denver Metro Area. Getting to the areas where the bighorns are often seen involves a walk or mountain bike ride of a mile or two up a gentle grade on a dirt road. Look for the sheep on the south-facing slopes at any time of the year, although they are more common in the winter.

DEADWATER SLOUGH, MIDDLE SALMON RIVER, ID—This area can offer excellent winter viewing of bighorns. To reach the area turn west off U.S. Highway 93 at North Fork in Central Idaho, on to Salmon River Road, viewing for the next 3.5 miles. Newland Ranch Picnic Area offers trail access to the habitat across the river.

MORGAN CREEK, ID—Bighorns are found in this area, north of Challis in Central Idaho, from November to May. To reach the location take U.S. Highway 93 north out of Challis and in about 8 miles turn northwest on Forest Road 55. The bighorns are usually found within the first five miles after leaving Highway 93.

GLACIER NATIONAL PARK, MT—Bighorns are often visible from the Highline Trail (access is from Logan Pass on Going-to-the-Sun Road), and also near Ptarmigan Lake in the Many Glacier area.

KOOKOOSINT SHEEP VIEWING AREA, MT—This area, eight miles east of Thompson Falls on Montana 200 in the northwestern part of the state, can be excellent during the rut in late fall and again in the spring.

SUNRIVER, MT—This area, 19 miles northwest of Augusta in west-central Montana, is home to 800 to 1,000 bighorns, one of the largest herds in the country. The bighorns are here all year, but during the winter and spring they can be seen much closer to the road.

WHISKEY BASIN, DUBOIS, WY—This part of the Wind River Range, a few miles southeast of Dubois in northeast Wyoming, is winter range to one of the largest bighorn herds in the country.

YELLOWSTONE NATIONAL PARK, WY—For those willing to walk several miles, the dirt road to the summit of Mt. Washburn is a reliable place to see bighorns. In winter, the slopes east of the road between Mammoth and Gardiner often have bighorns, and the confluence of Soda Butte Creek and the Lamar River in the northeast section of the park can also be good for bighorns during the winter.

MOUNTAIN GOAT
(Oreamnos americanus)

Just when you imagine that the goat you're watching must be clinging for dear life to a shred of ledge, it calmly lifts a rear foot and begins scratching an ear with it.
—Doug Chadwick, Montana wildlife biologist

"If we remain in the car, they may stay," I whispered to Cathy. It was our first trip up Mt. Evans, and the first time we had ever seen mountain goats. We desperately wanted to get some good photos before the animals were frightened away. As we got the big lens ready, a yearling walked across the road, stopped next to our front fender, and began licking the dirt next to the road for minerals. Several more followed and soon we were parked in the middle of the herd.

"This is ridiculous," Cathy said. "Our big lens is useless here." So we began photographing, one of us with a 90mm lens and the other with a 60-300 zoom. We got out of the car slowly, and the goats paid no attention to us. After grazing nearby for a few minutes, the goats made their way up a short *but near-vertical rock wall, leaving us to marvel at the ease with which they moved through this rocky terrain.*

MOUNTAIN GOAT FACTS

- Mountain goats are in the same family as cows, sheep, and goats (Bovidae).
- Mountain goats are more closely related to the goat-antelopes, such as the chamois and serow of the Old World, than they are to domestic goats.
- The males are called billies, females are nannies, and young are kids.
- Mountain goats have true horns that are never shed, similar to bison and bighorn sheep.
- Both the billies and nannies sport horns, making it very difficult to tell the sexes apart. When seen side by side, the male's horns are noticeably wider at the base than the female's.
- Breeding season is late November through December, and the males will sometimes fight to the death to protect a small, select group of females from rivals.
- Their horns are sharp, and they may not hesitate to use them. Even if the goats appear tame, give them plenty of room.
- Kids are born around the end of May.
- No other North American big game animal lives at such high altitudes. We have seen them above 14,000 feet on Mt. Evans in Colorado.
- Mountain goats often stay at high altitudes through the winter, depending on high winds to sweep the snow off forage. The guard hairs in their winter coat are hollow for greater insulation. So good is their insulation that if mountain goats did not shed their winter coat during the summer, they would die from overheating.
- Like bighorns, mountain goats will eat soil or lick up road salt for its mineral content.
- The soft, spongy material on the bottom of their hooves gives them a secure, firm hold on ice and smooth rock.

WHERE TO FIND MOUNTAIN GOATS

MT. EVANS, CO—Mt. Evans is by far the most reliable place in Colorado, and possibly the world, to see mountain goats. To reach Mt. Evans, take Highway 103 south from Idaho Springs (25 miles west of Denver on I-70) or west from Evergreen, and follow the signs. The road above Echo Lake is usually open from June through the end of August.

Look for mountain goats along the steep hillsides from several miles below Summit Lake all the way to the 14,262-foot top of Mt. Evans (this is also the highest paved road in North America). These goats may appear to be tame, and it can be easy to forget that they are wild animals and therefore unpredictable. Don't approach them too closely, and always leave them an escape route.

The goats were introduced here in 1961, and were originally considered an "exotic:" an animal that had not existed here before. Now there is some question about this theory. Recently rediscovered accounts from trappers and hunters, including Teddy Roosevelt, mention killing mountain goats in Colorado. This may mean that perhaps a native species has actually only been reintroduced.

BLACK MOUNTAIN LOOKOUT, ID—To reach this location, which is about 25 miles east of Orofino and north of the town of Headquarters in north-central Idaho, requires hiking about 4-1/2 miles one way. There is a large herd of mountain goats in this area that can be quite tame, and in July they concentrate around the lookout.

FARRAGUT STATE PARK, ID—This park is on Lake Pend Oreille, four miles east of Athol, in northern Idaho. The mountain goats roam the steep sides of Bernard Peak, across the bay from the park, and the only way to get a close view of them is by boat. The goats have become quite accustomed to boats, though, and will often remain close by if you sit quietly.

GLACIER NATIONAL PARK, MT—Glacier definitely offers some of the most spectacular scenery in which to see mountain goats. The area around Logan Pass on Going-to-the-Sun Road is a good place to start your search. The trail to Hidden Lake and the Highline Trail are two of the most reliable places to see goats. In the spring, they can be seen around Walton Goat Lick, on the south end of Glacier.

BISON
(Bison bison)

The buffalo was everything to us. When it went away, the hearts of my people fell to the ground, and they could not lift them up again.
—Chief Plenty-Coups of the Crow Indians

When I was about eight years old my family visited Yellowstone National Park, and among the many other things we saw was a large bison bull resting by the roadside. A semi-circle of photographers was busy recording the moment, and my brother, who was younger than I, slipped away from our parents and walked to the front of the crowd to get a close-up with his Instamatic. The crowd was already too close for safety, and as my brother approached, the bison bull stood up. My brother took the photo and walked away, never knowing how close he came to being gored and trampled.

BISON FACTS
- Bison are in the same family as cows, sheep, and goats (Bovidae).
- They are the largest land animal in North America. Large males can weigh as much as 2,000 pounds, and females can weigh half that much.

- Because of their short tempers, and because many observers underestimate their capabilities, bison are probably the most dangerous animals in the Rockies.
- Bison are faster than a race horse and amazingly agile. Be especially careful around large bulls and cows with calves. If the tail goes up (theirs, not yours), you're not in a very enviable position.
- Both sexes have true horns which are never shed.
- Males are called bulls, females are cows, and young are calves.
- Breeding season begins in late summer and lasts through early fall. Large bulls fight for dominance, but not necessarily to determine who mates with the cows.
- Calves, usually one and occasionally twins, are born in May and early June.
- Early Native Americans depended on the bison for their existence, and made use of the entire animal from it bones to its dung.
- In the early 1800s it was estimated that as many as 60 million bison roamed the interior of this continent. The bison population was once probably the largest single-animal-species biomass that this planet has ever seen. Settlers spoke of herds that extended for hundreds of miles.
- Between market hunting and a slaughter initiated to subdue the Indians, bison were nearly extinct by the 1870s.
- Bison use their massive heads to brush snow away to reach forage in the winter.
- Their habitat is long and short grass prairies, meadows and open forests.

WHERE TO FIND BISON

COLORADO—The Genesee exit off of I-70, about 15 miles west of Denver, is the best place in Colorado's Rockies to see bison. The animals may be on either side of I-70.

NATIONAL BISON RANGE, MT—Although its herd is managed intensely, like the one at Genesee, there are still lots of bison on this refuge in northwest Montana, and the access road should offer plenty of close views of them.

GRAND TETON NATIONAL PARK, WY—The bison here are free-roaming, and the best place to see them is between Snake River Overlook and Moran Junction.

Other free-roaming bison herds can be found in Wood Buffalo National Park in Canada; the Henry Mountains in southwest Utah; and the interior wilderness of Santa Catalina Island in Southern California.

YELLOWSTONE NATIONAL PARK, WY—Bison wander freely in Yellowstone, but the best places to see them, in both summer and winter, are usually the Hayden Valley, the hot springs basins from Old Faithful north, and the Lamar Valley.

Black Bear

BLACK BEAR
(Ursus americanus)
GRIZZLY BEAR
(Ursus arctos)

Statistically, the chance of being attacked by a grizzly in Yellowstone or Glacier is far smaller than being killed in a car crash on the way to the trailhead.
—Gary Gerhardt, *Rocky Mountain News*

As a child I visited Yellowstone with my family, and in less than an hour saw more bears than I have seen in the rest of my life. They were roaming among the traffic jams, peering into car windows, and sitting like beggars by the side of the road. People were trying to take pictures of them with their children, or make them do tricks like dogs—grizzly bears and black bears alike.

Since then I have seen grizzly bears twice. Both times in Yellowstone, and both times the bears were several hundred yards away working the sagebrush flats intently, trying to put on enough fat to survive the winter. Recently, there have been conflicting reports on the status of Yellowstone's grizzlies. Depend-

ing on which report you read, because of park policy (removing garbage from bears' diet, removing/destroying problem bears, allowing intense human activity in good bear habitat), Yellowstone's grizzly population is either dwindling toward extinction, or it's stable and healthy. Which is closest to the truth is anyone's guess. All I know is that seeing the bears roaming the sagebrush meant infinitely more to me than seeing them in the circus-like atmosphere that once existed in Yellowstone.

BEAR FACTS

- Both belong to the bear family (Ursidae).
- Both are classified as carnivores, although meat does not form the bulk of their diet except in unusual circumstances (if carrion is present, or fish are running in large numbers).
- Males are called boars, females are sows, and young are cubs.
- Male black bears can weigh up to 600 pounds, and females up to 350 pounds.
- Male grizzly bears can weigh up to 1,000 pounds, and females up to 550 pounds.
- Black bears have tapered faces, relatively large ears, and no muscular hump over the shoulders. Grizzlies have a dished-in face, small ears, and a very evident hump over the shoulders. Grizzlies also have much longer claws, and if you can notice that, you're probably too close.
- Black bears are good tree climbers. Grizzlies are not as proficient, probably because of their long claws.
- Black bears breed in June and July. Grizzlies breed from mid-May to mid-July. In both species the embryo does not implant in the female's uterus until five or six months after conception.
- Bears usually enter dens in October or November. They are not true hibernators. During their winter sleep their body temperature drops very little, and they can be roused from their winter lethargy. Though their metabolic rate remains comparatively high, they do not urinate or defecate for almost six months.
- The gestation period is only six to eight weeks. Cubs are born in January or February, weighing only about a tenth as much as a human baby.
- The bears emerge from their dens in April or May, and the females will have from one to four cubs. Not only do the males have nothing to do with raising the cubs, they will often kill the cubs if given the chance. Females with cubs do not tolerate the presence of males.
- Both black bears and grizzlies can be any color from black to blonde.

- Black bears are found in every state in the country, except Hawaii.
- At one time grizzlies ranged from the Central Plains to the Pacific Coast, and from the Arctic Ocean down to Arizona, New Mexico and Texas. Today, except for one that recently escaped from an exhibit in Oregon, they are restricted to Alaska, Canada, and the northern Rocky Mountain states.

WHERE TO FIND BEARS

For the most part bears are shy and elusive, and there is no place in the lower 48 states where you can depend on seeing them. If you do find them, do not approach them on foot, especially grizzlies, without first making out your last will and testament. It wasn't until the advent of firearms that man got the upper hand in human-grizzly encounters.

In recent years, at least two photographers have been killed trying to photograph grizzlies at close range. Approaching them not only places your life in danger, but also endangers the bear for it will surely be killed in retribution.

Grizzly Bear

COLORADO—In Rocky Mountain National Park there are no grizzlies, and black bears are seldom seen. There may be grizzlies in the San Juans in southwest Colorado (one was killed there in the 1970s years after they were supposedly extinct in Colorado), and people are looking for conclusive proof that they still live there.

GLACIER NATIONAL PARK, MT—If you don't mind walking, the Granite Park Chalet is one of western North America's safest places to view grizzly bears. It is a 7.6 mile hike along the Continental Divide from Logan Pass on Going-to-the-Sun Road to the chalet, and the chalet overlooks Bear Valley. Most summer evenings a ranger with a spotting scope is on duty. Overnight accommodations and meals at the chalet are by reservation only. (In 1993 the chalet was closed for repairs; call the park before visiting.) In autumn, grizzlies can sometimes be seen feeding on the snowberries above timberline along Going-to-the-Sun Road. They may also be seen above timberline in the Many Glacier area on the east side of the park.

YELLOWSTONE NATIONAL PARK, WY—Black bears tend to be found more in densely forested areas, and grizzlies in more open areas, but these rules have many exceptions. Grizzlies are often found near the Fishing Bridge Campground on Yellowstone Lake, especially when the trout are spawning. In the fall, grizzlies can sometimes be seen foraging on the sagebrush flats of Hayden Valley and from Tower Junction south to Dunraven Pass. In 1992, a couple of two-year-old grizzlies spent about two weeks close to the road below Dunraven Pass, in spite of everything that park personnel could do to discourage them. Those two bears were photographed by nearly every professional photographer and half the amateurs in the country during those two weeks.

GRAY WOLF
(Canis lupus)

Wolves lead violent lives. Of 110 examined along the Tanana River in Alaska in 1976, 56 had survived one or more traumatic injuries, incurred mostly, it was thought, in hunting moose. A four-year-old male, with healed fractures of the front left leg, two ribs, and the skull, was in fair to good condition.
—Barry Lopez, *Of Wolves and Men*

WOLF FACTS
- Wolves belong to the dog family (Canidae).
- At one time wolves were found from coast to coast on this continent. They ranged almost as far south as Mexico City, and as far north as Greenland.
- Their pelage (hair) may be any color from black to almost pure white, including slate blue, chocolate brown, ocher, cinnamon, gray and blond.

- An average gray wolf weighs about 80 pounds, and wolves weighing more than 120 pounds are rare. The largest wolf on record was a 175-pound animal killed in Alaska in 1939.
- Breeding takes place in February or March, and the pups are born in April or May.
- Normally there are four to six pups in a litter, but litters may range in size from one to thirteen. Pup mortality is high—60% or higher in most cases.
- Wolves have long legs and enormous paws for their size. A 90-pound wolf leaves tracks four inches wide and five inches long, more than twice the size of the tracks of a malamute of the same weight.
- Wolves can bite with a pressure of about 1,500 pounds/square inch compared to about 750 pounds/square inch for a German shepherd. This allows wolves to break open almost any bone they encounter.
- Wolves are pack animals. During the summer they may split up and hunt in pairs or even alone, but in winter they need the pack to survive.
- The pack may have anywhere from two or three animals to 15 or 20. There is an authenticated report of a pack of 36 wolves in Alaska, but packs larger than 25 are rarely reported.
- The social structure of the pack is all-important. Wolf pups raised without a pack adapt very poorly to life in the wild.
- In each pack there is usually an "alpha" (or dominant) male and an "alpha" female. There is only one breeding pair of wolves in each pack, and it is usually the alpha pair.
- Wolf packs are often led by females.
- Two- and three-year-old females are often faster than males of the same age, making them important hunters.
- Adult wolves express a strong interest in the pups, and make no effort to snatch food from them, or keep them from feeding on a kill. They will also bring food to members of the pack who are too old or injured to hunt.
- Adolph Murie, who spent many years studying wolves in the wild, wrote that the strongest impression he had of wolves (members of the same pack) was their friendliness toward each other.
- When howling, wolves harmonize rather than sing the same note, creating an impression of more animals howling than there actually are.
- Wolves are great travellers with tremendous endurance. One observer followed two wolves who broke trail through five feet of snow for 22

miles before laying down to rest. Wolves on Isle Royale National Park (Michigan) average 30 miles a day during the winter. Adolph Murie watched a pack in Alaska make a daily round of about 40 miles while the female was denning.

- Wolves do not get hungry the way humans do. A wolf's feeding habits and digestive system are adapted to a feast-or-famine existence. They often go three or four days without food, but when they get the opportunity, they can eat 1/5 of their body weight (20 pounds of meat for a 100-pound wolf).
- Wolves need to drink lots of water to prevent uremic poisoning, for a high meat diet produces lots of urea.
- Wolves are not the ruthless killers that wolf-haters say they are. A study done by wildlife biologist L. David Mech shows how complicated the relationship is between wolves and their prey. Out of 160 moose judged to be within range of hunting wolves, 29 were ignored; 11 eluded detection; 24 refused to run and were left alone. Of the 96 moose that ran, 43 got away immediately; 34 were surrounded but not harmed; 12 made successful defense stands; 7 were attacked, and 6 of those were killed while the last one was wounded and abandoned.
- In Wood Buffalo National Park (Canada), an observer watched three healthy bison and a lame one lying in the grass. As wolves approached, the three healthy bison ignored them, but the lame one appeared agitated. When one wolf approached within 25 feet the lame bison stood on wobbly legs to face them, giving away its weakness. It seems that both hunter and hunted play a role in prey selection.
- The Nunamiut Eskimos believe that during winter a healthy adult wolf can run down any caribou it chooses. It doesn't always do this, for reasons known only to the wolf, and maybe the caribou.
- Wolves will kill each other, usually when a territorial trespass is involved. Strangely behaving wolves may be killed by their own pack members.
- Studies show that wolves prey largely on the aged, the diseased, or the very young. But wolves also take animals in their prime, and occasionally they kill in excess of what they can eat. The truth is, they will likely try to kill any animal that presents itself at a disadvantage.
- It's been many years since most of the Central Rockies have known the howl of a wild wolf, but the times may be changing. Wolves from Canada have colonized the area around Glacier National Park. In 1992, in north-

western Wyoming, a hunter shot what he thought was a coyote, and which genetic studies have proven was a wolf. Although studies are currently underway to determine the feasibility of reintroducing wolves to Yellowstone National Park, the animals may not have waited for approval. In 1993, an amateur video was made of an animal in Yellowstone National Park that certainly resembled a gray wolf.

COYOTE
(Canis latrans)

There's an old Indian saying that when the last man is gone, the song dog will still be here. No matter what happens, I'm convinced of that.
—Dwain Nelson, Bureau of Land Management, Vernal, Utah

A large group of cars was stopped ahead, and in Yellowstone that can only mean one thing: some sort of wildlife spectacle. We assumed our place at the end of the line, and looked around to see what was causing the commotion. It was a relatively small animal for Yellowstone, alone in a small meadow, and obviously intent on its hunting.

The coyote would take a few cautious steps with its head cocked to one side, crouch down for a few seconds, leap high in the air, and come down forepaws and jaws first. After a few seconds of wrestling in the grass, the coyote would lift its head up with a still-struggling vole in its jaws. In the five attacks we were able to watch, the coyote never missed.

COYOTE FACTS

- Coyotes are members of the dog family (Canidae).
- At about 25 pounds, coyotes are as big as a medium-sized dog.
- The word *coyote* is a corruption of the Aztec *coyotl*, which means barking dog.
- They breed in mid-February to early March, and pups are born in late April or early May. They may mate for life.
- If the coyote population in an area is low, the females will breed at a younger age, and have larger litters.
- Coyotes are one of the few species that have increased their range as civilization has expanded westward. At one time coyotes only existed west of the Mississippi, but in spite of relentless persecution, coyotes have expanded their range to include every state but Hawaii.
- One of the reasons for this expansion is that coyotes are opportunists. They will eat anything from big game to insects to berries. Some suburbanites have found that letting their pets run around loose is also of great benefit to the local coyote population. Domestic cats and dogs have become just another link in the food chain. It's hard to blame the coyotes, though. After all, they were here first, and we moved in with them.

WHERE TO FIND COYOTES

ROCKY MOUNTAIN ARSENAL, CO—Surprisingly, one good place is on the edge of Denver. See the notation under mule deer for information on arsenal tours.

ROCKY MOUNTAIN NATIONAL PARK, CO—Coyotes live in the park all year, but they are much easier to find in the winter. This time of year they are often seen in Horseshoe Park, Moraine Park and Beaver Meadows. During the summer they can be anywhere in the park, even above timberline.

YELLOWSTONE NATIONAL PARK, WY—This is probably the best place to find coyotes, especially in the winter. Look for them in Hayden Valley, along the Lamar River between Tower Junction and Soda Butte, Gibbon Meadow, Elk Park, Virginia Meadows, and along the Madison River from 7 Mile Bridge to Madison Junction.

RED FOX
(Vulpes vulpes)

In the fox, evolution has fashioned a creature for which every input is tuned to maximum sensitivity: for the fox there is the jolting image of the rabbit's blinking eyelid, the clamorous squeak of a mouse 20 meters off, the dreadful reek of a dog's day-old paw print.
—David MacDonald, British scientist and naturalist

The fox kit slowly approached Cathy with its nose extended, constantly sniffing the air, trying to discern what kind of creature she was. Cathy sat quietly, and the kit approached to within four feet of her. Then the vixen materialized out of the brush nearby, and our curious visitor ran back to mom to see what presents she had brought home.

It was indeed a special morning, but it was made even more unusual by the fact that this fox den was in an urban area. We could hear traffic over the sound of the nearby creek. We are finding that red foxes are proliferating in urban open spaces, and places of semi-civilization.

FOX FACTS
- Red foxes belong to the dog family (Canidae).
- At 8 to 15 pounds, red foxes are not much larger than a housecat. Their stunning pelage just makes them look larger.
- Red foxes are not always red. They can be black, silver, almost blonde, or any combination of these colors. A red fox, regardless of its color, has a white tip on its tail.
- Males are called dog foxes, females are vixens, and young are kits or pups.
- They breed in late January or early February, and males will fight for the right to pair with a female.
- After breeding the foxes select a den site, usually digging a hole in the ground, or using a hollow tree.
- The kits are born in mid-March, and their eyes don't open for 10 to 12 days. After about 5 weeks they leave the den for the first time. We have seen them as early as the first week of April.
- Red foxes will often use a series of dens, sometimes splitting the kits up among 2 or 3 different dens.
- Red foxes prefer a habitat of open woodland and meadow with water nearby.
- They do not compete favorably with coyotes.
- They are typically rare in the Rockies, although in 1993 biologists told of discovering a new subspecies of red fox that is living, year round, at 11,000 feet on the Beartooth Plateau east of Yellowstone.
- Trappers say you'll find more foxes per square acre in the city of Denver than you'll find anywhere else in the state.
- The red fox is one of the few canids that is a solitary hunter.
- Foxes reportedly will go out of their way to kill snakes, although they rarely eat them.

WHERE TO FIND RED FOXES

Red foxes are hard to find in the Rocky Mountains, although Red Rocks National Wildlife Refuge in Montana just west of Yellowstone National Park has a good population of them. The only places we've seen red foxes though, have been urban areas. They are becoming locally abundant along the eastern foothills of Colorado's Front Range.

Places like open spaces, cemeteries, golf courses, and irrigation canals can offer the best opportunities to see foxes at close range. For years Crown Hill Cemetery in Lakewood, a suburb of Denver, was probably the best place in the country to photograph foxes. In 1992, though, a pair of coyotes moved into the cemetery, and they have been killing and chasing off the resident red foxes. Places where we have seen red foxes include Walden-Sawhill Ponds in Boulder, Fairmount Cemetery, Crownhill Park, the Wheatridge Greenbelt in the Denver metro area, and along Fountain Creek in Colorado Springs, Colorado.

MOUNTAIN LION
(Felis concolor)

There was the huge carcass of a recently killed elk. It's neck had been broken and its antlers driven 9" into the ground. An animal weighing 150 pounds had destroyed one weighing 800.
—Wildlife researcher Maurice Hornocker, "Learning To Live With Mountain Lions," *National Geographic* 12/92. Founder/director of the Hornocker Wildlife Research Institute, Idaho.

MOUNTAIN LION FACTS
• Mountain lions are members of the cat family (Felidae).
• Also called cougar, puma, screamer, panther, king cat, painter, ghost walker and catamount.
• Males can weigh up to 160 pounds, and females up to 100 pounds.
• Although these animals can breed any time of the year, most kittens are born in the spring. The male remains with the female only as long as she is receptive to mating.
• At one time mountain lions had the most extensive range of any native American mammal. Except for a handful of individuals waging a losing

battle against civilization in southern Florida, the mountain lion is now restricted to remote, rugged habitat in western North America.
- They hunt by stalking and leaping on their prey, not by long chases. Deer are a large percentage of their diet, although elk and smaller animals are also taken.
- Mountain lions are one of the few cats that have round pupils.
- In the past, mountain lions were rarely seen, and almost never photographed in the wild. And even today you could spend all your life in good lion country and never see one. Things are changing, though. All along the eastern foothills of Colorado's Front Range the deer are invading the suburbs, and the mountain lions are following them. The only two photographers I know who have photographed mountain lions in the wild, did so in open-space areas on the western edge of Denver.

Lions are at their highest levels in years in Colorado, and juveniles are being forced to seek new territories closer and closer to our urban centers. Often these lions are too young to be expert at taking deer, so they turn to pets. Talk about easy pickings. Just like the coyote situation, though, don't blame the mountain lions. They were here first, and we moved in with them.

Bobcat

BOBCAT
(Lynx rufus)
LYNX
(Lynx canadensis)

It's not in the bobcat's nature to stand and fight unless it's cornered, but when it does, a 30-pound bobcat can make mincemeat out of a 90-pound hound.
—Michael O'Brien, Wildlife researcher

BOBCAT AND LYNX FACTS
- Both are members of the cat family (Felidae).
- Weighing about 20 pounds, bobcats are barely twice the size of a domestic cat. Lynx are slightly larger, and weigh up to 35 pounds.
- Bobcats are found in every state but Indiana in the contiguous 48 states. Lynx are rare south of the Canadian border, and are restricted to areas that receive lots of snow.

- Lynx have longer tufts of their ears than bobcats, and the dark and light pattern on their faces is not so prominent.
- Bobcats are the feline equivalent of a jack-of-all-trades, and are very adaptable. Lynx are intimately tied to their chief prey animal, the snowshoe hare.
- Lynx populations rise and fall with the snowshoe hare population. Bobcats will simply pick another item from the menu if one prey species is in short supply.
- It is believed that there are more bobcats in this country now than there were in Colonial times. This is a benefit of being largely ignored. Bobcats are not valuable enough to be a game animal, and not destructive enough to be seriously persecuted.
- Bobcats cannot tolerate domestic cats, and if humans force the two species to coexist, domestic cats are going to suffer.

Lynx

LONG-TAILED WEASEL
(Mustela frenata)
SHORT-TAILED WEASEL
(Mustela erminea)

In winter, weasels continually teeter on the brink of starvation. If they don't eat every 24 hours or so they may die.
—Mikael Sandell, Professor of Wildlife Ecology, Univ. of Agricultural Sciences, Umea, Sweden

WEASEL FACTS
- Naturally, weasels are in the weasel family (Mustelidae), and like all members of this family found in the Rockies, they have paired anal glands that release a powerful, malodorous musk.

- It can be difficult to tell these species apart. The long-tailed weasel has a tail that is more than half the length of its head and body. The short-tailed weasel, or ermine, is generally smaller and its tail is less than half the length of its head and body. In its summer coat, the short-tailed weasel has light-colored feet, and the long-tailed weasel has dark-colored feet. In the winter both species turn white except for a black tip on their tail (in the extreme southern part of their range they don't change colors in winter). People mistakenly refer to both species as ermine when they are in winter white.
- Both species breed in mid-summer, but the embryos don't implant on the female's uterine wall until mid-winter. The young are born in the spring.
- A weasel's heart beats several hundred times a minute.
- A weasel's life expectancy is only about 18 months. To compensate for such a short life span, the females are sexually mature and fertile at 10–12 weeks of age (sometimes even as early as six weeks of age).
- Weasels have a reputation for being vicious, but often they are simply hungry. Their long, slender shape radiates heat quickly, and they need to consume 1/4 to 1/3 their body weight in food each day. The human equivalent would be that of a grown man needing to eat 50 pounds of food each day or starve to death.
- If food is readily available, weasels will often kill more than they can eat, and stockpile the rest. They will often kill prey several times larger than themselves.
- Native Americans used the white, winter pelts of both long-tailed and short-tailed weasels to decorate robes and warbonnets. European kings used the winter pelt of the short-tailed weasel as a badge of royalty.
- Short-tailed weasels are relatively rare in the central Rockies, and long-tailed weasels are common. In Rocky Mountain National Park, the long-tailed weasel is probably the most abundant carnivore.
- Long-tailed weasels can be found from the ponderosa pine forests of the foothills up to alpine tundra. One of the best places to find them can be around pika colonies, for they are one of the few predators that can follow pikas through their underground labyrinths.

NORTHERN RIVER OTTER
(Lutra canadensis)

Otters may be the only animal that can kill a beaver in its den.
—Adrian Forsyth, *Mammals of the American North.*

Otters are famous for their playful personalities. One winter's day on Yellowstone Lake we watched an otter with a fish teasing a coyote. The otter would lay the fish on the ice, and apparently pay no attention to it. The coyote would cautiously approach, and when it was within 10 feet of the fish, it would lunge forward. By the time the coyote's feet hit the ice, the otter had grabbed the fish and disappeared through a hole in the ice. A few minutes later though, the otter and its fish were back, teasing the coyote again.

OTTER FACTS
- Otters are members of the weasel family (Mustelidae).

- Otters mate in the summer, but the fertilized egg doesn't implant in the uterine wall until winter. The babies are born in the spring, with an average litter size of three.
- Immediately after the young are born, the adult male is evicted for a short time. He will return some weeks later to help raise the young.
- Otters are marvelously adapted to life in the water, and are capable of swimming half a mile underwater without coming up for air.
- Because fish are a large part of the otter's diet, some fisherman have no love for them. However, otters tend to eat "rough fish" like suckers which may actually improve the fishery.
- In addition to fish, otters will eat crayfish, frogs, and even water-loving mammals like muskrats and beavers.
- Otters have luxurious fur that not only is thick and soft, it is extremely durable. The guard hairs of most furbearers become brittle in severe cold. Only otters and wolverines have hair that retains its pliability in bitter cold.
- Habitat destruction is the biggest threat facing otters today.
- A pair of otters will often work together driving a school of fish into the shallows where they can be caught easily. Large catches are carried to land to be eaten, and smaller ones are consumed as the otter floats on its back.
- Otters have highly sensitive facial whiskers that may aid in locating their prey in murky water.
- An otter's eyes are near the top of its head and, like a crocodile, it can float just below the surface and still keep an eye on things.

WHERE TO FIND RIVER OTTERS

River otters are always on the go, and they have an almost unlimited home range. Seeing them is simply a matter of being in the right place at the right time.

Otters have been reintroduced in Colorado in the Piedra and Dolores Rivers in the southwest part of the state, and in the Colorado River in Rocky Mountain National Park. Probably the best place to see them though, is Yellowstone National Park. The Madison, Lamar, Firehole and Gibbon Rivers are all good places to look for them. During the winter, we've also seen them near the West Thumb Geyser Basin on Yellowstone Lake.

Another place where they can be found in the winter is Wade Lake, just west of Highway 287 and northwest of Yellowstone National Park in Montana.

In Idaho some good areas for otters are Musselshell Meadows (about 12 miles southeast of Weippe in north-central Idaho on Forest Road 540) and Deadwater Slough on the Middle Salmon River (from North Fork in west-central Idaho go west on the Salmon River Road .6 miles to the Newland Ranch Picnic Area).

STRIPED SKUNK
(Mephitis mephitis)

A hunter sees a mule deer buck sprayed by a skunk. The muley immediately sheds his antlers before slinking off down the valley. Clearly, he knew he would not be mating that year.
—Wayne McLoughlin, "A Reason To Fear," *Field & Stream*, 12/92 from the Phoenix Sage, September 20, 1891

SKUNK FACTS

- Skunks are in the weasel family (Mustelidae), and like all mustelids in the Rocky Mountains they have paired anal musk glands. The skunk's musk glands have earned the animal considerable notoriety, for they have evolved into a fearsome defense weapon. The genus name, *Mephitis*, means noxious smell.
- There are five species of skunks in North America, but the striped skunk is the most common in the Rockies.
- Skunks can spray up to 16 feet, and their aim is accurate for 6-10 feet. The musk not only smells terrible, it causes temporary blindness and extreme pain if sprayed in the eyes.
- Before spraying, the skunk usually gives some warning. It may arch its back, click its teeth, stamp its front feet, and then it does a handstand. When it does a handstand, it's time to be somewhere else.
- It spite of their unparalleled defense, some animals still manage to prey on skunks. The most successful of these is the great horned owl. The owl has a big advantage over most carnivores, though, for it has no sense of smell.
- Skunks mate in March or April, and an average of five helpless young are born in May or June. The young are weaned within two months, and by fall they are independent.
- Skunks are not picky eaters. Their diet includes birds' eggs and nestlings, small mammals, frogs, berries, and many insect species. Skunks are significant predators of hornets, wasps, and bees. They will dig into a nest, grab the stinging insects as they emerge, and kill them by rolling them between their tough palms.
- Striped skunks are common in many parts of the Rockies, but because they are largely nocturnal, they are rarely seen.
- Skunks are another species that do well in urban areas, and the first skunk that many people see is the one living under their house.

Marten

AMERICAN MARTEN
(Martes americana)
FISHER
(Martes pennanti)

The marten is so sensitive to changes in its environment that it is officially classified as an indicator species.
—Steven Buskirk and Henry Harlow, "Hunting For An Elusive Hunter," *National Wildlife*, December 1989

Cathy and I have been lucky enough to see pine martens on three different occasions in Rocky Mountain National Park, but the most memorable time was in Wild Basin in the southeast corner of the park. As we were taking a few photos around camp, Cathy hissed to get my attention. I looked up, and there was a marten rummaging through the remains of our breakfast, only 15 feet away.

For several minutes he explored the entire camp, paying not the least bit of attention to us, before he decided that our breakfast hadn't been all that great. What can I say—we were backpacking. If the morning hadn't been so cloudy, we could've taken pictures of the marten with its head inside an M&M bag.

MARTEN FACTS
- Pine martens and fishers are in the weasel family (Mustelidae).
- Pine martens are about the size of a small cat, and fishers are two to three times that large. In addition to being smaller than fishers, pine martens can be distinguished by their orange throat patch, and by a dark mark above each eye that looks like a vertical eyebrow.
- Pine martens are the most arboreal of the weasels.
- Fishers are seldom seen, and require large tracts of wilderness for their survival. Pine martens don't require as much wilderness as fishers, but they are dependent upon old-growth forest. Pine martens do not hibernate, and their fur doesn't have the insulating quality of pronghorn hair or

Fisher

red fox fur. Because of this, they have to rely upon the deadfalls, snags and hollow trees found in old-growth forests to protect them from winter's cold. Also, pine martens will not cross a clearing as large as 25 yards, even for an obvious source of food. A wide road through their habitat effectively fences them out of part of their territory.

- Both pine martens and fishers have semi-retractable claws, and hind feet that can swivel 180 degrees. Both of these traits are of tremendous value in climbing trees.
- Fishers are famous for their ability to prey upon porcupines. People used to think that fishers flipped them over, and attacked the porcupine's belly. Researchers now believe that fishers kill the porcupine by repeatedly attacking its unprotected head.
- Pine martens have a varied diet that includes squirrels, mice, pikas, birds, rabbits, berries, and sweets like honey. Seeing one with an M&M bag on its head told us right away that it had a sweet tooth.

AMERICAN BADGER
(*Taxidea taxus*)

Badgers can burrow faster than any other mammal, and one can easily bury itself faster than a man can dig it out with a shovel.
—*The Audubon Society Field Guide to North American Mammals*

BADGER FACTS
- Badgers belong to the weasel family (Mustelidae).
- Badgers usually weigh between 10 and 25 pounds.
- They are especially suited for digging with their long, stout claws and massive shoulders.
- Their eyes are small and have a special membrane to protect them from dirt.

- Badgers show considerable sophistication in their hunting technique. When hunting ground squirrels, they will often plug every entrance but one to the ground squirrel's underground den. Then they just have to dig the squirrel out.
- Badgers have thick, hard-to-pierce skin, are hard to kill, and are extremely ferocious when harassed. Do not corner one.
- They have a vast territory, and consequently, do not return to the same den every night. They simply take a few minutes to dig a new one.
- They can be found in a variety of habitats. Almost anywhere from prairie to alpine tundra can be home for badgers as long as there are plenty of ground squirrels, chipmunks, prairie dogs or gophers for them to prey upon.
- In tribal lore, the badger was a medicine man who knew which roots were good for treating certain ailments.

WOLVERINE
(Gulo gulo)

In Western literature, the first mention of these animals was made by Olaus Magnus, a Swedish bishop. In 1555 he wrote that in the Arctic there were three vicious monsters: a giant octopus, a sea serpent, and the wolverine.
—Bill Gilbert, "What To Do If a Demon of the North Comes a-Callin?" *Smithsonian*, 3/93

WOLVERINE FACTS
- Wolverines are the largest members of the weasel family (Mustelidae), and can weigh more than 50 pounds.
- They have an impressive set of claws, and are good at climbing trees.
- A wolverine can be identified by its stocky, bear-like appearance, by its blond eyebrows and sideburns, and by a blond, lateral stripe which runs from behind its shoulder to its rump.

- Wolverines are solitary animals. They breed in summer when the males roam in search of females. As with many species in the weasel family, the embryo does not implant and develop until winter, and the young are born in mid-spring. In most cases the young disperse the following autumn.
- Although originally known as the "Demon of the North," researchers and trappers no longer consider the wolverine demonic. It's a tough, opportunistic creature doing the best it can in a harsh environment.
- Some researchers claim that the badger and the wolverine are, pound for pound, the strongest of our native mammals.
- Naturalists in Denali National Park in Alaska once watched a 40-pound wolverine drag a Dall sheep carcass weighing more than 120 pounds for nearly two miles.
- A trap was set at a ski resort in the Canadian Rockies where a wolverine was continually breaking in and stealing food. The trap was chained to a 75-pound log. They caught the wolverine, but only after it climbed a wall of the building, broke through a barred window and escaped, all while dragging the trap, chain, and log.
- Audrey Magoun, while working on a doctoral dissertation on wolverines, spent five years live-trapping them in Alaska's Brooks Range. The live trap was constructed of 11-gauge steel cyclone fencing such as is used in military installations. Several times wolverines escaped by pulling apart the heavy mesh. One time a fox was captured in one of the traps. A passing wolverine was able to pry apart the fencing enough to reach in, kill the fox, and pull it out, piece by piece.
- Wolverines survive the winter by storing food during the warmer months. Some of the caches get quite large. In Siberia a wolverine cache contained 20 fox and 100 ptarmigan carcasses. Although wolverines will hunt and kill their own prey, they depend to a large extent on carrion, and they are also called the "hyena of the north."
- Although they are not particularly fleet, wolverines have almost unsurpassed endurance. There are cases where a wolverine has been pursued by air or snow-machines, and has run for 40 miles without stopping. If food is scarce, a wolverine may travel 60 miles or more in its daily search.
- Your chances of seeing a wolverine in the Central Rockies are slim. Even in Alaska wolverines have never been common. They are solitary creatures of the wilderness. The lower 48 states have never been more than marginal range for wolverines, but there are still a few around. As recently as the late 1970s wolverines have been seen in Rocky Mountain

National Park. Cathy and I think we saw one above timberline in Colorado's Holy Cross Wilderness, but the animal was a long distance away, and we didn't have binoculars. Glacier National Park, in northern Montana, offers the best opportunity to see wolverines in the Central Rockies.

COMMON RACCOON
(Procyon lotor)

Raccoons have great manual dexterity, and their name is thought to come from the Algonquin *aroughcoune*, which means "he who scratches with his hands."
—*The Audubon Society Field Guide to North American Mammals*

The only one we've ever seen in the Rockies appeared to be on its way to the Safeway in Estes Park before sunrise one morning.

RACCOON FACTS

- Raccoons are in the family Procyonidae, which has only three North American members, the raccoon, the ringtail, and the coatimundi.
- Raccoons mate in February. During this time the male moves in with a female for a week, and then he's off looking for more females.
- The raccoon's species name, *lotor*, means "washer," though they don't wet their food for hygienic reasons. Much of their food is found in or near the water making it appear like they're washing it. Also, raccoons identify many things by touch, and some researchers believe that their sense of touch is enhanced when their fingers are wet.
- Raccoons are renowned for their intelligence, and their learning ability ranks somewhere between cats and rhesus monkeys.
- Crayfish are a favorite food, but raccoons will eat almost anything.
- Raccoons prefer the riparian areas of the Rocky Mountain foothills to the conifer forests and tundra of the high peaks. An inability to tolerate the cold winters of the boreal forests is one of the few limits to their success at colonizing North America.
- Since the 1950s, raccoon numbers have greatly increased in the lower regions of Rocky Mountain National Park. One explanation may be that raccoons are very tolerant of human activity.
- There are several reasons raccoons do well in urban areas. Raccoons are semi-arboreal, and the trees we plant give them places to hide. Also, garbage cans and dog dishes make ideal places for raccoons to scavenge.
- Because they are almost strictly nocturnal, raccoons can be difficult to find even when they are numerous.

AMERICAN BEAVER
(*Castor canadensis*)

The beaver looks like some kind of a mythical beast put together out of a grab bag of parts belonging to other animals.
—Hope Ryden, author, *Lily Pond—Four Years with a Family of Beavers*

Beavers can play a key role in riparian habitat management. South of Breckenridge, a small community wanted several small dams built to improve water quality. A contractor wanted $20,000 to build these dams. Two beavers were transplanted instead, and they built seven environmentally friendly dams for free.

BEAVER FACTS
- Beavers are rodents and are the only species in their family (Castoridae).
- Beavers are the largest rodents in North America, usually weighing between 45 and 60 pounds, but some have been trapped weighing more

than 100 pounds. The only rodent in the world that is larger is the South American capybara.
- Beavers are believed to mate for life. Their breeding season is from late January to late February, and a litter of one to eight kits is born four months later.
- On this continent, only man can alter the environment to the extent that beavers can. Their dams may be 100 yards long, and they will sometimes dig canals as well.
- In ponds, beavers will usually build a lodge of sticks and mud with an underwater entrance to serve as their den. If they live in a river, beavers will usually dig a den in the riverbank, and it will also have an underwater entrance.
- Generally, two mature beavers and their offspring from the past two years will inhabit a territory. When the young reach two years of age they usually set out to establish their own territories. It is during these travels that beavers suffer their greatest losses to predation.
- A beaver will often slap the water with its tail to warn of intruders approaching.
- They do not hibernate. They establish a "cache" of green sticks underwater where they are able to feed on them through the winter.
- Beavers have a split toenail on their hind feet that is used to both comb their fur, and rub oil into it from a gland at the base of their tail, keeping the fur waterproof.
- Beavers played a big role in the early development of the Rockies. In the early 1800s high prices for beaver pelts created a rush to the west that was second only to the gold rush.
- Beavers are numerous enough now that they sometimes become a nuisance by flooding roads or chopping down cultivated trees. Of course, people moving into what has always been the beaver's backyard doesn't help matters.

WHERE TO FIND BEAVERS

Beavers are common in the Rocky Mountains, but they are largely nocturnal, and you can seldom count on seeing them during the daylight. Autumn is probably the best time to see them in the daytime, if they're going to be out at all, for they are busy preparing for winter. In Rocky Mountain National Park, good places to look for them are the beaver ponds in Hidden Valley below the old ski area and along the Colorado River in the Kawuneeche Valley, especially in the Timber Creek Campground area.

Other places to look for beavers in the Rockies include the Snake River at the south end of Grand Teton National Park in Wyoming, the oxbow on Lower McDonald Creek on the west side of Glacier National Park in Montana, and the Chain of Lakes area along the Coeur d'Alene River in Idaho (18 miles east of Coeur d'Alene, turn south on Idaho 3 to Rose Lake; look on both sides of the highway for the next 13 miles).

COMMON PORCUPINE
(Erethizon dorsatum)

"How do porkies mate?"
"Carefully."
—Old joke.

PORCUPINE FACTS
- Porcupines are rodents, and they are the only North American species in their family (Erethizontidae).
- The beaver is the only North American rodent larger than the porcupine.
- A porcupine's 30,000 quills are modified hairs. Porcupines cannot shoot their quills. The quills are usually stabbed into the victim with a good swat of the tail.
- The quills are covered with microscopic, backwards-pointing barbs making removal very difficult and painful. The quills also absorb fluid and swell up, adding to the problem. Once imbedded, the quills will continue to work their way inward.

- The quills may have antibiotic properties which inhibit infection; probably an adaptation that protects the porcupine in the rare instances that it sticks a quill into itself.
- Native Americans used the quills, both dyed and natural, in decoration.
- Porcupines mate in the fall. A single offspring is born after a gestation period of 205 to 217 days, almost as long as a moose. Because of their long gestation period though, the young are born fully developed, and can care for themselves soon after birth.
- Porcupines have evolved one of the slowest reproductive rates of all mammals. Their excellent defense system results in such low mortality, though, they don't need to reproduce rapidly.
- Porcupines are born with soft quills, but within 30 minutes the quills become hard and dangerous.
- Porcupines do not hibernate.
- In spring, porcupines feed on the base of trees for the sugary inner bark. In winter, they feed on the tender branches of the upper canopy. Attracted by salt, they will gnaw on anything that has been perspired on. Outdoorsmen have found paddles, boots, gunstocks, and axe handles destroyed by porkies. Porcupines also have a sweet tooth, and will chew through brake lines or radiator hoses for the sweet but poisonous taste of ethylene glycol or brake fluid.
- We have found porcupines everywhere from scrub oak thickets in the foothills to spruce forests above 11,000 feet. We even found one hiding in a prickly pear cactus in the desert outside of Tucson, Arizona. One morning as we were driving through the Kawuneeche Valley in Rocky Mountain National Park before sunrise we almost ran over four of them in the space of two miles.

COMMON MUSKRAT
(Ondatra zibethicus)

It would take an Olympic swimmer to compete with a muskrat, which can swim up to 3 miles an hour.
—Laima Dingwall, *Muskrats*

MUSKRAT FACTS
- Muskrats are rodents in the mouse family (Muridae), and they are in the vole subfamily (Arvicolinae). At 1-1/2 to 3 pounds they are the largest of the voles.
- *Ondatra*, its genus name, was originally its Iroquois name.
- Muskrats are named for two prominent musk glands at the base of their abdomens which are used during breeding seasons to stake out territories and attract mates.
- They produce 2 litters a year. Though the young are born helpless, they can swim within 2 weeks.
- They do not hibernate as many rodents do.

- Muskrats either build lodges out of cattails and bulrushes or excavate dens in the bank. Both have underwater entrances and resting platforms above water level. They will also use abandoned beaver lodges. On one occasion, they were observed using a beaver lodge while the beavers were living there, too.
- Muskrats are able to close their lips behind their large incisors, which allows them to prune vegetation underwater.
- They have partially webbed toes and a long, laterally flattened tail, both of which aid in swimming.
- Muskrats can stay submerged for 17 minutes.
- Vegetation forms the bulk of their diet, but they will also eat frogs, clams, crayfish, small turtles, and even young waterfowl.
- Females will kill other females and their offspring to gain control of a den. Males will fight other males for territories.
- It is the most valuable semi-aquatic furbearer on the continent. In the Netherlands, the government is forced to trap thousands of muskrats each year to protect their precious dikes from muskrat burrows. Since the government has also outlawed the sale of fur there, they now have to burn the animals they trap.

YELLOW-BELLIED MARMOT
(*Marmota flaviventris*)

Marmots can be host to the tick that carries Rocky Mountain Spotted Fever.
—*The Audubon Society Guide to North American Mammals*

MARMOT FACTS

- Marmots are rodents in the squirrel family (Sciuridae). They are closely related to the woodchucks of eastern United States.
- The yellow-bellied marmot gets its name not from being a coward, but from the color of its belly, which is covered with yellow or golden fur.
- It is one of two species of marmots found in the Rocky Mountains. Yellow-bellied marmots are found as far north as central Montana, and hoary marmots are found from central Montana up into Alaska. The two species look similar, but the hoary marmot has silver-colored guard hairs on its upper body giving it a grizzled appearance. The hoary marmot can also weigh up to 20 pounds, almost twice as large as the yellow-bellied.

- Marmots prefer open areas, but they can be found anywhere from evergreen forests to alpine tundra. They live in burrows or dens, usually under or around rock piles. They are adaptable, however. A Montana population has been discovered that uses hollow trees in a cottonwood grove as den sites.
- Marmots live in loose colonies made up of extended family units, and they will give a high-pitched, warning whistle if danger threatens.
- They spend the summer stuffing themselves with green vegetation, trying to build up enough fat to survive the winter.
- Marmots are true hibernators, and in winter their body temperature may drop to 36 degrees F.

WHERE TO FIND MARMOTS

Marmots are common in many parts of the Rockies. On some high peaks that receive lots of traffic (Mt. Richtofen in Rocky Mountain National Park and Notch Mountain in the Holy Cross Wilderness come to mind immediately). The marmots are not shy about inviting themselves to dinner.

In Rocky Mountain National Park, Forest Lakes Overlook and the Rock Cut area, both high on Trail Ridge Road, are good places to look for yellow-bellied marmots. Mt. Washburn in Yellowstone National Park also has a good population. To see hoary marmots, the area around Logan Pass in Glacier National Park is a good bet.

Abert's Squirrel

ABERT'S SQUIRREL
(Sciurus aberti)
RED SQUIRREL
(Tamiasciurus hudsonicus)

In addition to pine cones, red squirrels will also eat a variety of fruits, bird's eggs, young birds, and fungi, even Amanita mushrooms, which are deadly to humans.
—*The Audubon Society Field Guide to North American Mammals*

SQUIRREL FACTS
• These animals are the two common tree squirrels in the Rockies, and, of course, both are in the squirrel family (Sciuridae).
• Abert's squirrels are recognized by the extra long tufts on their ears. Their color can be black, blonde, gray, or something in between.
• Red squirrels, or chickarees, can be any color from rust-red to gray. Their white eye ring is a good identifying mark.
• At one time it was thought that Abert's squirrels were tied to ponderosa pine forests. Recently, they have been found in other habitats, but it's rare to find Abert's squirrels outside of ponderosa pine habitat.

- Red squirrels seem to prefer the denser spruce/fir, Douglas fir, and lodgepole pine forests. A good sign that red squirrels are in the area are "middens," large piles of cone scales and cores, the leftovers from eaten pine cones. These middens can be 20 to 30 feet across and a foot deep.
- A large part of an Abert's squirrel's diet is supplied by the ponderosa pines it lives in—seeds, buds, inner bark, and young male cones. Abert's squirrels will also eat berries, fruits, fungi, and some carrion. Like most rodents, they will also gnaw bones and antlers for their mineral content.
- Red squirrels are common throughout the Rockies from New Mexico to Canada. Abert's squirrels prefer old-growth ponderosa pine forests and are found from northern Colorado south to New Mexico and Arizona. Good places to see them include the east side of Rocky Mountain National Park (Beaver Meadows Visitor Center is a good place), Lookout Mountain Visitor's Center just west of Denver and north of I-70 (follow the signs), and Elk Meadow a few miles northwest of Evergreen on the west side of Highway 74.

Golden-Mantled Ground Squirrel

GOLDEN-MANTLED GROUND SQUIRREL
(*Spermophilus lateralis*)
CHIPMUNK
(*Tamias species*)

All chipmunks have an amazing capacity for storage in their cheek pouches. An eastern chipmunk can hold six chestnuts in its cheek pouches, and each chestnut is nearly as large as the chipmunk's head.
—Merebeth Switzer, *Chipmunks*

GROUND SQUIRREL AND CHIPMUNK FACTS
- Both chipmunks and golden-mantled ground squirrels are rodents in the squirrel family (Sciuridae).

- There are at least five species of chipmunks that can be found in the Rockies, and they can be very difficult to tell apart as they scamper about. Also, the shape of their penis bone (baculum) often figures prominently in distinguishing between chipmunk species. In this guide they will all be called simply chipmunks.
- Chipmunks can be distinguished from golden-mantled ground squirrels by their stripes. On chipmunks, the stripes pretty much stretch from the tip of their nose to the base of their tail. Golden-mantled ground squirrels are usually larger and bolder than chipmunks, and their stripes only run between their shoulders and hips.
- Both species hibernate during the winter, although they may awaken from time to time to eat from stored food.
- Both species are vital to the ecology of North America, serving as an important food source for many meat eaters.

Chipmunk

WYOMING GROUND SQUIRREL
(*Spermophilus elegans*)

These squirrels are called "picket pins" because of their habit of standing upright at attention, making them look like the picket pins cowboys tied their horses to.
—*The Audubon Society Field Guide to North American Mammals*

GROUND SQUIRREL FACTS
- Ground squirrels are rodents in the squirrel family (Sciuridae).
- Until recently the Wyoming ground squirrel was considered the same species as Richardson's ground squirrel (*Spermophilus richardsonii*), and older publications reflect this earlier taxonomy (the science of classifying living organisms).

- Richardson's ground squirrel is an animal of the open plains, and before the coming of the plow these creatures outnumbered prairie dogs. Their capacity for storing cultivated seeds was their undoing. The cheek pouches of one ground squirrel contained 162 oat seeds, 140 wheat seeds, and almost 1,000 wild buckwheat seeds.
- The Wyoming ground squirrel prefers high valleys or parks between mountain ranges.
- Besides plants and their seeds, their diet includes many insects, especially grasshoppers, crickets and caterpillars. They will also eat members of their own species that have been killed by cars. Protein is hard to come by in a vegetarian diet.
- Wyoming ground squirrels are colonial in favorable habitat, and they are true hibernators.
- These ground squirrels can be hard to find, but when you find them there are often lots of them around. Two places in Colorado where they are easy to find are near Painted Rocks Campground north of Woodland Park, and in North Park, especially Arapaho National Wildlife Refuge in north-central Colorado.

WHITE-TAILED PRAIRIE DOG
(Cynomys leucurus)

Prairie dogs manipulate the soil, increase plant diversity and create higher forage quality. Wildlife and cattle preferentially feed on the forage that grows on these prairie dog colonies.
—Ted Williams, "No Dogs Allowed," *Audubon*, 9-10/92.

PRAIRIE DOG FACTS
- Prairie dogs are rodents in the squirrel family (Sciuridae).
- They were given the name "dog" because of the high-pitched bark they give as a warning signal.
- Black-tailed prairie dogs (*Cynomys ludovicianus*) are the ones the settlers encountered while crossing the prairie, and they do not occur in the mountains. White-tailed prairie dogs are slightly smaller than black-tailed, and they have a white tip on their tail instead of a black one.
- White-tailed prairie dogs are usually found in high valleys or parks between mountain ranges in the central Rockies.

- White-tailed prairie dog towns are relatively small—200 individuals or less, compared to those of black-tailed prairie dogs. In Texas, it was estimated that some 400 million black-tailed prairie dogs lived in a single prairie dog town that took up 25,000 square miles of prairie.
- White-tailed prairie dogs do not have the elaborate social system that black-tailed prairie dogs do.
- Prairie dogs of all species have been intensely persecuted. Research is now showing that prairie dogs, by fertilizing and aerating the soil, are beneficial to the surrounding grassland.
- Good places to find white-tailed prairie dogs are Arapaho National Wildlife Refuge south of Walden in north-central Colorado, and Hutton Lakes National Wildlife Refuge south of Laramie, Wyoming.

SNOWSHOE HARE
(Lepus americanus)

Snowshoe hares are preyed upon by every conceivable predator. Even red squirrels kill and eat the babies.
—Mark O'Donoghue and Susan Stuart, "Hare-Raising Encounters," *Natural History*, 2/93.

SNOWSHOE HARE FACTS

• Snowshoe hares are lagomorphs rather than rodents, and they are in the rabbit and hare family (Leporidae).

• Lagomorphs have an extra pair of upper incisors behind the ones you can see. This is one of the features that differentiates lagomorphs from rodents.

- The snowshoe hare gets its name from its extra-large hind feet. In winter it also grows stiff hairs on the sides of its hind feet that aid in staying on top of deep snow.
- Snowshoe hares are famous for turning white in the winter and brown in the summer. This phenomenon is initiated by decreasing daylight in the winter and increasing daylight in the summer. If the first snows are late, the snowshoe hares will be very conspicuous in their white pelage.
- Hares are born fully furred, and with their eyes open. Rabbits are born hairless, and with their eyes closed. Snowshoe hares can move about within hours of their birth.
- Young hares separate from their mother each day, spending the day alone in hiding, and returning to a central location to nurse. After feeding they disperse again. This behavior is thought to reduce predation.
- Snowshoe hares are can leap 12 feet in a single bound, but they depend more on hiding under cover than fleeing for protection.
- Snowshoe hares maintain a series of trails through their territories to aid in escape from predators. They will actually groom the trail, clipping twigs and branches, so they can run as fast as possible down these trails when they need to.
- Although most of their diet is vegetation, snowshoe hares will eat carrion. Some have become a nuisance to trappers by stealing bait.
- Snowshoe hares are fond of dust baths, and although they are generally solitary animals, several will sometimes gather at choice dust bath sites.
- Snowshoe hares are generally common in the boreal forests, especially in the northern Rockies. Look for them feeding beside the road early in the morning, in such parks as Rocky Mountain, Yellowstone, Grand Teton, and Glacier.

MOUNTAIN COTTONTAIL
(*Sylvilagus nuttallii*)

The male cottontail doesn't stay with his mate very long. She usually turns on him a few days after mating and chases him out of her territory with vicious bites.
—Merebeth Switzer, *Rabbits*

COTTONTAIL FACTS
- The cottontail is a lagomorph in the rabbit and hare family (Leporidae). Like all lagomorphs, it has an extra pair of upper incisors.
- The mountain cottontail, also called Nuttall's cottontail, is the most common rabbit in the Rockies.
- Like all rabbits, its young are born hairless and with their eyes closed.
- Because of predation, cottontails have one of the highest mortality rates of any mammal: 85 percent of them never reach their first birthday. To combat this assault, cottontails have an incredible reproduction rate. They can bear 4 to 5 litters per year, and they average 5 young per litter.
- Cottontails have a short gestation period of only 28 days, and they mate again right after the young are born.

AMERICAN PIKA
(Ochotona princeps)

Thomas Nuttal described their call as "a slender but very distinct bleat, so like that of a young kid or goat" that he was astonished when "the mountains brought forth nothing much larger than a mouse."
—*The Audubon Society Field Guide to North American Mammals*

PIKA FACTS

- Pikas are related to rabbits and hares rather than to the mice and voles that they resemble, and they belong to the pika family (Ochotonidae).
- Like all rabbits, pikas have an extra pair of upper incisors behind the ones you can see.
- It is called "Little Chief Hare" by Native Americans, and this is reflected in its species name (*princeps* means *chief*).
- The name *pika* comes from the Tunga people of northeast Siberia, and was originally pronounced *peeka*.

- Like all rabbits, and unlike many rodents, pikas do not hibernate. They spend the summer cutting and drying vegetation, just like farmers, and live off this "hay" during the winter. By the end of "haying" season, a pika's many hay piles would fill a bathtub.
- Pikas are restricted to huge rock piles or talus slopes bordering open meadows at high elevations. In Colorado they can be found from above 14,000 feet down to 8,500 feet. Up near the Canadian border their range extends down to about 5,500 feet.
- Contrary to earlier reports, recent findings show that pikas cannot tolerate high temperatures. Pikas are so well insulated in their little fur coats that six hours in the sun at 70 degrees will kill them. This is why they are restricted to the higher elevations.
- It's usually easy to determine if pikas are in the area. The electronic "eek" or "beep" that is their warning and territorial call will usually sound from several different locations as you approach the area.
- The breeding season is from April to June, and the young are born 30 days after mating. Soon after giving birth, the female mates again. However, she will only give birth to the second litter if the first one does not reach weaning age.
- Pikas are relatively common in rock slides (if there is a good food supply nearby, and if it's high enough above sea level) throughout the Rockies. The jumble of rocks around the Rock Cut on Trail Ridge Road in Rocky Mountain National Park is a good place to listen and look for them.

BIBLIOGRAPHY

1. Ulrich, Tom J., *Mammals of the Northern Rockies*.
2. Zeveloff, Samuel I., *Mammals of the Intermountain West*.
3. Forsyth, Adrian, *Mammals of the American North*.
4. Armstrong, David, *Rocky Mountain Mammals*.
5. Craighead, Karen, *Large Mammals of Yellowstone and Grand Teton National Parks*.
6. Lopez, Barry Holstun, *Of Wolves and Men*.
7. Fischer, Hank and Carol, *Montana Wildlife Viewing Guide*.
8. Carpenter, Leslie Benjamin, *Idaho Wildlife Viewing Guide*.
9. Gray, Mary Taylor, *Colorado Wildlife Viewing Guide*.
10. *The Audubon Guide To North American Mammals, 1980*.
11. Dingwall, Laima, *Muskrats*, Nature's Childrens Series.
12. Switzer, Merebeth, *Rabbits*, Nature's Childrens Series.
13. Switzer, Merebeth, *Chipmunks*, Nature's Childrens Series.

ABOUT THE AUTHORS

Cathy and Gordon Illg are photojournalists specializing in nature and outdoor recreation. This is their first book, although their work has appeared in such publications as *Outdoor Life*, *Owl*, *Wildbird* and *Colorado Outdoors*. For the past twelve years Cathy and Gordon have been traveling the byways of the Rockies, diligently gathering data for this book. Although, at the time, they thought they were only looking for wildlife.

Wendy Shattil and Bob Rozinski, whose photography has appeared in such magazines as *Audubon*, *National Wildlife*, and *National Geographic World* in addition to their own books, were the *BBC Wildlife Magazine's* "Photographers of the Year" in 1990. Their work has been exhibited at the Boston Science Museum, the Carnegie Museum in Pittsburgh, the Field Museum in Chicago, as well as museums throughout Europe.

FIELD NOTES

FIELD NOTES

FIELD NOTES

FIELD NOTES